During the 1980s, cocaine use grew enormously in the United States and increasingly in Europe. It is thought that some 35 tonnes were consumed worldwide in 1982, rising to 70 tonnes in 1985 and to 270 in 1988. By the end of the decade, there were an estimated six million regular users in the United States alone and over 20 million occasional users. A new drug has come on the market too, a derivative of cocaine known as crack, which is cheaper and more concentrated and has the effect of creating almost immediate addiction.

The rise in demand for cocaine has been accompanied by high levels of violence. Enormous profits are made from the drug. In Colombia, a powerful elite, known as the "drug barons", has emerged. They control the most profitable part of the cocaine trade: the processing and distribution of the coca leaf, and are prepared to kill to retain their control. The huge profits made by the Colombian drug barons enable them to build their own private armies and buy large tracts of land. By the late 1980s, the drug barons had created a virtual state within a state.

Members of the Colombian political and economic establishment have mixed feelings about the rise of the cocaine mafia. As part of a Third World country with limited resources, many have tacitly welcomed American dollars earned by the drug barons, and some politicians have even used drugs money to build their political power. Some members of Colombia's most traditional political and military establishment have actually formed alliances with drugs traffickers to create paramilitary groups to kill their common enemies: members of left-wing opposition movements and trade unionists as well as leaders of protest movements.

But there are many Colombians who have deeply opposed the mafia's growing power. In August 1989, the drug barons of Medellín arranged for the assassination of a leading opponent of the cocaine trade, Luis Carlos Galan. This assassination led the Colombian government to take its strongest measures yet against the power of the drugs mafia, with support from the US government. A virtual cocaine war broke out, in which hundreds have died.

At stake is the authority of the Colombian government. But there are many other issues too. Why have people become involved in producing the drug in the first place? Is it possible to eradicate cocaine production and distribution using the army? Should governments try to stop the demand for cocaine rather than its supply?

The story of cocaine

The story of cocaine begins with the coca leaf. For centuries the Indian communities used the leaf as a medicine and in religious ceremonies. Today it is mass-produced as a drug and consumed in the rich countries of Europe and North America.

The history of the coca leaf

Coca is one of 13 alkaloids produced from the coca leaf. The cultivation and consumption of the coca leaf in the Andean region of Latin America dates from some 3,000 years before the birth of Christ. Its name derives from one of the most advanced cultures of upper Peru, the Aymara, who called it *kkoka*, meaning shrub or bush.

Consumption of coca was widespread among the majority of native cultures of Latin America before and after the Spanish conquest; it was an integral and much revered part of their way of life. They believed coca was a gift from the gods. The Incas, who established an empire centred in present-day Peru in the 13th century, believed they had received it from *Mama Ocllo* and *Manco Capac*, the divine founders of the empire.

The coca leaf played an important role in religious ceremony and ritual. Many powers were attributed to it: healing powers, power to make men more virile and the power to create visions and enhance understanding of the natural world.

△ The Guambiano people are one of a number of surviving Indian groups in the Colombian Andes. Chewing coca leaf continues to play a part in the life of these communities.

◁ About 300-500 kg of coca leaves are needed to make one kilogram of cocaine. The leaves contain the alkaloid cocaine, which has to be separated out in order to produce the drug in a pure form. Bolivia is reputed to produce leaves containing the highest levels of the alkaloid.

Coca use

The leaf was consumed in various ways. Often it was made into a liquid and drunk to cure stomach complaints and chest problems. It was also chewed together with leaves of the *guarumo* plant, which contains the lime necessary to release the narcotic alkaloid in the coca leaf. Until the Spanish conquest, this usually took place only on festival days or at special ceremonies.

After the conquest, the practice became more widespread. As well as a small amount of the narcotic cocaine, the coca leaf contains essential oils and some minerals and vitamins. It therefore provided sustenance as well as a very mild stimulant against the harsh Andean climate and the brutal working conditions imposed on the natives by the Spanish. Today an estimated three to four million peasants and miners in the Andean highlands chew coca to help them deal with cold, hunger and exhaustion.

In the late 19th century, Europeans started to use the drug we now know as cocaine as an anaesthetic, and discovered its medicinal value. Then, in 1886 in Atlanta, Georgia, an American entrepreneur launched a new drink which used the coca leaf without the cocaine. The drink was called Coca-Cola. Even today, nearly 300 tonnes of coca leaves are legally imported into the United States from Peru for the manufacture of Coca-Cola extract.

Cocaine also came to be used as a narcotic in the last century, and Arthur Conan Doyle's fictional hero, Sherlock Holmes, gave it some notoriety. Demand for cocaine as a drug increased gradually, but remained relatively small until the latter part of the 20th century.

The drug culture

In the 1960s many young people in Europe and the United States started to use illegal drugs, mainly marijuana. The region around Santa Marta in Colombia became a major producer of marijuana, and some Colombians gained experience in the drugs trade, although North Americans rather than Colombians controlled it. Marijuana production was in fact stamped out by the Colombian Army under American pressure at the end of the 1970s. (Today, the United States grows 55 per cent of the US marijuana consumption within its own borders.) During the 1970s, demand for cocaine grew steadily in the United States. Gradually the Colombian mafia, who had been involved in marijuana dealing and other illegal activities, moved into this highly profitable new business.

5

Growing the coca

The story of how coca becomes cocaine begins with the impoverished peasant communities of the Andean countries of Peru and Bolivia, as well as Colombia. Peru and Bolivia are by far the most important sources of coca leaf, while the Colombians control the most lucrative stages of the production process: refining, smuggling and wholesaling. The peasants who grow the coca leaf receive only the tiniest fraction of the profits involved in the cocaine trade. Still, for the peasants of Chapare in Bolivia, the Upper Huallaga valley of Peru and the eastern region of Colombia (see map page 32), it offers an unparalleled opportunity for making money. The coca plant produces three to six harvests each year for up to 40 years. It is easily cultivated and flourishes in areas unsuitable for most other crops, and also grows in isolated areas where any other crop would be very expensive to transport to the market. In these regions, the state has often completely neglected the needs of the peasant farmers. Credit to buy fertiliser, seeds and technical assistance has been unavailable. But the cocaine middlemen are only too eager to offer all these aids to peasants willing to grow coca.

No other crop could offer the peasants the kind of income available from coca. In 1985, a Peruvian coca farmer could earn US$7,410 per hectare. This was ten times the per hectare earnings of a cocoa farmer and 91 times those of a rice farmer. Although coca leaf prices fell in the late 1980s, in December 1986 a coca farmer in the Bolivian Chapare could earn about US$2,600 a year from a single hectare of coca. This was more than four times the return from a hectare of oranges or avocados, the most competitive traditional crops, and more than four times the average Bolivian's income in 1986.

From coca to cocaine

The next stage in the cocaine chain is when middlemen acting for traffickers pick up coca leaves from the farmer and transport them to nearby laboratories. These laboratories convert the leaves into paste. This requires a considerable number of workers who literally tread the leaves (they are called *pisadores*, which means tramplers). The leaves are then soaked in kerosene solution to remove the cocaine. The conversion of the coca paste to cocaine base, and finally to cocaine hydrochloride, has traditionally been done outside the coca-growing areas, and the Colombians have dominated the processing.

△ Jorge Luis Ochoa, head of the Ochoa clan of drug traffickers and a leader of the Medellín cartel with Pablo Escobar. He was captured by government forces on 22 November 1987, but a Colombian judge released him a few weeks later. Bribery and intimidation of judges have prevented the courts from bringing the important traffickers to justice.

▷ Money and crack seized by New York police after a drugs raid. In London, official figures show that the police made 43 seizures of crack in the first two months of 1990. This compares with 138 for the whole of 1989. Cocaine and crack addiction may well become a major problem in Britain.

An international problem

In the mid-1980s, Latin American cocaine traffickers earned at least US$5 billion a year from the sale of cocaine on international markets. Experts suggest that the rate of profit (how much it costs to produce compared to how much the product sells for) ranges from 50 to 80 per cent. There are few activities which could generate such a large return. In October 1987, *Fortune* magazine put two leading Colombian drug traffickers, Pablo Escobar Gaviria and Jorge Ochoa, among the 20 richest men in the world. The Colombian government released pictures of their luxury homes which had gold taps and luxurious fittings.

Prices dropped during the late 1980s because the United States had more cocaine than demand called for. This encouraged the traffickers to look more to European markets. Britain is now increasingly concerned at the amount of cocaine coming into the country, and the growing use of crack. In April 1990 Margaret Thatcher, the British prime minister, called an international conference to give urgent international attention to the problem. The conference revealed the many differences which still exist on how to tackle the drugs problem.

△ Pablo Escobar's ranch, *Napoles*, shows the money he expends to satisfy his extravagant taste. In addition to his antique car collection, Escobar has built a private zoo.

The roots of the crisis

The outbreak of the drugs war in 1989 turned Colombia into one of the world's hotspots. But the rise of the cocaine trade, and the violence associated with it, can only be explained by looking at the evolution of the deeper crisis of Colombian society and state. This chapter looks at Colombia's history and the roots of the crisis.

Colombia today is a racially mixed country of Indian, Spanish and African people. The origins of this mix of people lie in the history of the indigenous peoples who lived in the area for at least 12 thousand years before the Spanish conquest in the 16th century. The origins of the native population were Asiatic and Oceanic (from the Pacific Islands). By the 16th century there were an estimated three to four million Indian people in the area of present-day Colombia. This population had reached different levels of development. Primitive and nomadic tribes inhabited the Amazon jungle, while in the highland areas, people such as the Quimbayas, Tumacos, Calimas and those of San Agustin, had fairly advanced forms of agricultural life. The Muiscas of the eastern highlands and the Tairona of the Atlantic coast were most advanced of all. However, there were no vast and sophisticated Indian empires in Colombia, such as the Incas' empire in Peru.

The Spanish conquest

The Spanish began their conquest at the beginning of the 16th century, using the Cauca and Magdalena rivers as arteries along which they could explore the interior. They founded San Sebastián de Uraba in 1509, Popayán in 1537 and Santa Fe de Bogotá in 1538. In the process, the indigenous population was decimated by the violence of conquest, their lack of resistance to new diseases brought by the conquerors, and the harsh conditions of slavery the Spanish imposed on the people. Today, only about 500,000 pure Indians remain in Colombia, though most Colombians have some Indian blood. The third racial group, the Africans, were brought by the Spanish as slaves to work in gold mines, on ranches and as servants. Today they constitute about six per cent of the Colombian population.

Throughout the 16th, 17th and 18th centuries the Spanish dominated the region, which in 1739 became the Viceroyalty of New Granada. They imposed their language, religion, institutions, customs and traditions on the native people. They extracted gold, and gave huge estates to the conquerors and their descendants. The estates were worked by Indian and African peoples, who lived in misery and virtual slavery.

Results of the conquest

By the end of the 18th century the area of present-day Colombia was still a backward and impoverished region. Its wealth had been shipped to Spain, and that which remained in the country was highly concentrated in the hands of the great landowners, merchants and mineowners. Transport was hazardous and arduous, communication was poor, and regional isolation and regional interests were strong. Opposition to Spanish control of trade and administration grew and led many of the local-born elite, or creoles, to join a rebellion in 1781. This rebellion also unleashed the anger of the poor and native people against the Spanish who had dispossessed them. Fearful of this movement from "below", the creole elite joined the Spanish authorities in crushing it. However, by the beginning of the 19th century, this creole elite had organised its own independence movement.

Spanish rule created a highly unequal society. Present-day Colombia still manifests those inequalities and this remains a source of much social tension. Independence freed the local-born creole elite from Spanish rule, but it did not bring freedom to the peasants.

△ An engraving portrays the conquest of Peru by the Spanish conquistador, Francisco Pizzaro. It depicts the cruelty of the conquerors towards the Indian population.

◁ The pre-Colombian Indians were skilled goldsmiths and produced wonderful gold artefacts. Many were melted down by the Spanish, but some which survived are on display at the Museum of Gold in Bogotá. This raft with a royal figure and servants is one of the prize pieces of the collection.

Independence but no nation

The war of independence between the creole elite and the Spanish colonial government was prolonged and bloody, complicated by conflicts within the elite which led the rebellion. Simon Bolivar led the independence struggle, and was the first president of a federation of Andean states, known as Gran Colombia. It was established in 1819 after the decisive battle of Boyaca.

Rivalries and disputes led to the defeat of Bolivar's vision of a strong state and a united Latin America, and in 1830 the federation broke up. In the years that followed, disunity, instability and outright war characterised the new republic of Colombia. During the 19th century there were eight general civil wars, 14 local civil wars, countless small uprisings and three *coups d'etat*.

The elite was divided over questions of economic development, forms of government and the role of the Catholic Church in society. By the middle of the 19th century two political parties had emerged to represent the different views on these issues, the Conservative and Liberal Parties. Both parties have dominated Colombian political life up to the present day.

Conflict and compromise

There was not much difference between the two parties, but a tradition of resolving disagreements through war began. Peasants were drawn in to fight for the large landowners and when they saw their relatives killed by the opposing party, they developed enmities and loyalties towards their own party which would fuel further wars. Curiously, however, two contradictory traditions were born in these years. On the one hand that of war and revenge, and on the other that of electoral life, reconciliation and compromise.

In between wars Colombia enjoyed a lively political life, establishing the political culture which has many democratic features: changes of government following elections, a congress (or two-house parliament), and a civilian rather than military tradition which distinguishes it from other Latin American countries, where the army seizes power from the politicians in a coup.

In Colombia the two traditional political parties had strong roots before the army was established on a professional basis (a process which began in the 1880s but was not completed until the 1940s). As a result, the army remained under the influence of political parties until the 1960s, when it gradually asserted its political autonomy.

△ Simon Bolivar with his troops. Bolivar is one of the great figures of Latin America's struggle for independence from Spain. He had a vision of a united Latin America with a strong and effective government. This was thwarted, however, by power struggles between local elites.

The Colombian Jesuit priest, Francisco de Roux, comments "it is a simplification to say that the Colombian people were aggressive from the start. Rather, what you find is a country where the political customs of the ruling class have led the people into war from the first days of the republic."

Federation of Gran Colombia 1820-30

Venezuela

Colombia

Ecuador

Brazil

Peru

Border disputes

Panama 1903

Venezuela

Colombia

To Colombia
from Ecuador
1922

Ecuador

To Brazil
from Venezuela
1904-5

To Peru
from Ecuador
1942

To Brazil
from Colombia
1904-5

Peru

Brazil

Colombia's weak state

Despite these political traditions the Colombian state was weak. Neither one of the two parties was able to defeat the other and assert its power. The country and its people were too poor for a strong central government to develop, which would have been able to control the fighting, and build the roads and communication systems essential for economic development. Other Latin American countries were able to find one or two export crops in the 19th century. A strong state was then able to establish itself around the interests of the group which produced the exports.

This did not happen in Colombia until the early 20th century. Although a government of National Reconstruction led by a Conservative, Rafael Nuñez, attempted in the 1880s to re-establish the authority of central government and the Catholic Church, Colombia ended the 19th century in the middle of its bloodiest civil war yet. Some 100,000 people died in the Thousand Day War (1899-1902).

Since independence, Colombia's ruling elite had fought to preserve its local bases of power rather than establish a strong state. The tradition of weak central government was, many decades later, to make it difficult for the state to deal with threats to its authority.

△ In the 19th and 20th centuries there were a number of border disputes between Colombia and its neighbours. But the most significant territorial change occurred in 1903, when the United States deliberately encouraged Panama to secede from Colombia. The United States was then able to build the Panama Canal and continue to increase its dominance over Central and South America. The United States is still a force in the region, both economically and militarily.

◁ A coffee-drying yard in the Camargo estate, San Nicolás, Colombia in the 1920s. Coffee growing and production were vital to the development of Colombia in the 20th century.

Land ownership

By the beginning of the 20th century, Colombia was one of the most backward countries in Latin America. Roads were poor and river transport slow. It took four to six weeks to travel from the Atlantic ports to Bogotá along the Magdalena river.

A small landowning elite enjoyed what wealth there was. During the 19th century this elite had extended its control over the land. Its huge estates were known as *latifundia*. Colombia had an extensive agricultural frontier. The Spanish had mostly settled on the high land of the west. Such land could only support a certain type of crop, and in order to grow new crops which might be in greater demand for export, it was important to move down the slopes to warmer climatic conditions.

Large landowners sought to gain control over the newly colonised land. In the process a battle began between them and peasant colonisers seeking a small plot to support their families, a conflict which still exists today. When the slopes were settled and the agricultural frontier moved to the lowland areas of the eastern plains in the 1950s, the battle continued and in the course of this struggle, coca growing became an instrument used by peasants to ensure the survival of the peasant economy.

The misery and backwardness of rural areas have been a source of social and political unrest in Colombia. The extreme concentration of land ownership has given local landowners considerable political as well as economic power. Local political bosses, known as *caciques*, have traditionally manipulated the peasants in favour of either the Liberal or Conservative Parties. The party bosses and landowners opposed any reforms which might have helped avoid the crisis of later years.

▽ A mule-pack train loaded with coffee on a mountain road in the Andes. Colombia's physical terrain made the transport of goods very difficult. Rail, road and river transport improved in the first decades of the 20th century and helped increase coffee exports. But as late as 1950 the World Bank stated that transport difficulties were still preventing economic development.

Coffee and the nation-state

There was one area of the country, however, where small farmers were able to settle alongside the larger ones, and where gold production had enabled a fairly wealthy merchant class to emerge. This was Antioquia in the northwest. This region was to provide the impetus for Colombia's economic growth and modernisation in the 20th century. It was here that coffee growing expanded after the destruction of the large estates in the east during the Thousand Day War in the early 1900s.

Coffee became so important to Colombia that by 1930 it accounted for 70 per cent of exports. This made Colombia dependent on virtually one crop and therefore very vulnerable to price changes and disruptions in the world market. But with the foreign currency it earned, Colombia could begin to set up its own industries, importing the equipment and skills which other more advanced countries had already developed. The state now had an income which enabled it to begin the process of modernising communications, roads, ports and railways in order to facilitate exports, and to build a banking system. Some peasants now moved into urban areas and the towns grew.

Social change and political control

Coffee production brought many social and economic changes with it. Struggles for land grew more acute, particularly in areas where large coffee estates still dominated and peasants wanted the right to grow the "golden bean" themselves. Workers began to organise as well, and the 1920s saw many labour struggles, particularly among the key river and railway workers, and those in the oil sector and banana plantations where American money had recently been invested. A massacre of over 1,000 striking banana workers in Ciénaga on the Caribbean coast shook the country in 1928.

But despite all the changes taking place, the political system remained the same. The two traditional parties predominated, controlled by the old elite but sustained by the loyalties they still commanded among the people. Politics was the preserve of this old elite. Conservative regional landowners could easily guarantee the vote of their peasants, and the Conservative Party dominated the rural areas and the state until 1930. Even though peasants fought landowners for access to land, and workers fought bosses for higher wages, their movements enjoyed only a brief period of independence from the traditional parties.

13

Party conflicts

In 1930 the Liberals courted the new urban vote and were able to win that year's election. Since many Colombians were impoverished and excluded from the country's development, President Lopez Pumarejo recognised the need for the state to provide more social welfare programmes. However, this rumour of reform provoked immediate hostility from the country's deeply conservative political establishment, and particularly from the Conservative Party itself.

Within that party, an extreme right-wing current was growing, influenced by General Francisco Franco's Falangist government in Spain and supported by the Catholic Church. Within the Liberal Party, a leader emerged who did not look to his fellow party members for support, but who appealed directly to the people. Jorge Eliécer Gaitán tried to mobilise the rural and urban poor against the "oligarchy", as he called the wealthy elite which dominated political life in both parties. His aim was to modernise the country and promote economic growth, which would be shared out on a more equal basis.

By the late 1940s Gaitán had become the leader of the Liberal Party and was gaining popular support. However the "oligarchy" did not want him in power and in 1948 he was assassinated in the capital city of Bogotá.

Civil war

The people in the city went wild, and took out their anger and frustration in a wave of destruction known as the "*Bogotazo*". The country was now deeply divided. The people were confused; their expectations had been raised by Gaitán and then crushed. They had no leaders or movements of their own and thus could look only to the traditional parties. The Conservatives who now controlled the government organised a terrible repression against the Liberals, using terror tactics to kill and maim their opponents. The Liberals began to raise guerrilla armies to defend themselves.

The scene of the action moved to the countryside, where certain villages attacked other villages in an orgy of violence. The years that followed are known to history as *La Violencia*. An estimated 200,000 people died in this civil war, which did not finally end until 1964. The end came with the killing of most of the "bandits", former guerrilla leaders who had refused to accept the peace terms negotiated by the party leaders.

△ The *Plaza de Bolivar* (Bolivar Square) in Bogotá in 1948 just before the killing of the liberal leader, Jorge Eliécer Gaitán. In the foreground are members of the Colombian Army in dark uniforms and white helmets.

La Violencia
"The month of October (1949) marks one of the most abominable in the history of the decomposition of Colombia. The hamlet of Ceilan in Bugalagrande is attacked, set on fire and sacked. The bandits leave about 150 dead, some of them burned. Immediately afterwards, 27 citizens of San Rafael are murdered; their bodies thrown into the river stain the waters a pure scarlet."
La Violencia en Colombia by Germán Guzmán, Orlando Falf Borda and Eduardo Omaña Lima; published in 1963.

The National Front

Party leaders realised that they had unleashed a wave of horrendous violence. There was a danger that in the course of the struggles taking place, the peasants might revolt against the landowning class as a whole. In addition, it was evident that if Colombia was to develop, peace between the parties must be restored.

The first attempt to halt the violence was in 1953, when a number of party leaders encouraged the army to take over the government. But the new military president, General Gustavo Rojas Pinilla, tried to move away from the parties and build his own power base. Party leaders then organised a movement to overthrow him in 1957 and reached an important agreement in 1958 between themselves which would have a profound impact on the future of the country.

By this pact – called the National Front – the parties agreed to alternate the presidency between themselves for 16 years (1958-74) and to divide all cabinet, congressional, judicial and local government posts equally between them. A constitutional reform in 1968 opened elections to other parties and eliminated the division of posts in Congress (1974) and locally elected bodies (1970).

Competitive presidential elections were not held until 1974. But even after this date, the majority party had to offer the runner-up party a suitable number of representatives in government. It was not until 1986 that President Virgilio Barco Vargas, a Liberal, attempted to govern without the Conservatives. The two parties between them continue to dominate political life and are likely to do so well into the future.

△ General Gustavo Rojas Pinilla appears on the balcony of the presidential palace shortly after seizing power in a coup in June 1953. Many members of the elite saw a brief period of military rule as the only way to end the violence between the traditional parties.

▽ President Barco (who served from 1986-90) was the first Colombian president since before the National Front to form a government based on "one party in power, one party in opposition".

Problems with the pact

This agreement secured peace between the parties, neither of which had to fear exclusion from government by the other. But it had a number of negative effects. People now saw less reason to vote as the parties had already agreed on who would be in government. Loyalties to the two parties declined. This also affected other institutions, notably the army, which now became stronger. The parties themselves were also divided. Mostly this was not due to conflicts over policies or ideas, but because regional party bosses fought each other for power within the party. The party bosses bought votes with offers of jobs. Corruption became rife in the parties, the government and the judiciary, where posts depended less on ability than on party membership and friendships with particular party bosses. The political system was more closed than ever, excluding many who no longer felt represented by the two traditional parties. Colombia's political and legal system was in crisis even before the drug barons emerged to corrupt it further.

During the 1960s, 1970s and 1980s Colombia underwent tremendous economic growth, which was accompanied by an extraordinarily high level of violence. The causes of this violence are a subject of much discussion in the country and many theories have been put forward. Colombian violence is of two kinds: criminal violence, which may have economic or social roots, and political violence.

△ The tall office blocks and modern flats of Bogotá can be seen behind the grinding poverty of the shanty-towns. The two Colombias, rich and poor, exist side by side.

△ Scavenging for survival in Bogotá. An estimated 30,000 Colombians make a living from the rubbish of the major cities. People collect refuse in little carts or on their backs and sell it for recycling. Some of the poor resort to crime to make a living; some get involved with the drugs trade or commit theft and a few even turn to violence in their desperation.

◁ An official survey in 1988 of 13 towns showed that 32 per cent of the towns' population of 11.4 million live in poverty, despite the fact that Colombia has a relatively advanced economy for a Third World country. This is particularly serious for the children. The cities are full of abandoned children, or street children, forced to survive by begging and stealing in the crime-ridden streets of the big cities.

Poverty, crime and violence

At least some of the explanation of Colombia's high level of violence lies in the pattern of economic development (see page 30), which has excluded millions. In particular, there has been the very rapid growth of cities without government planning or support to the incoming families. The state has been unwilling or unable to help the poor, or to force the wealthy to accept the need to provide social welfare by taxing their wealth. In the cities many have turned to crime, which has led to violence. By 1973, Colombia had one of the highest murder rates in the world: 19.8 murders for every 100,000 inhabitants. Smuggling, petty theft, kidnapping and extortion were all rife in the cities before the illegal drugs trade developed. Outside the cities, struggles over resources such as gold and emeralds generated extraordinary violence, such as in the 1970s in the emerald-producing region of western Boyaca, where 600 people died in a war for control of the emerald mines.

However it was not only the poor who engaged in criminal activity. Within the judiciary and the civil service, corruption was widespread. The legal profession has been unable to deal with the level of crime because of lack of resources, bribery and intimidation. The rise of cocaine enormously increased the level of crime and violence, but it mainly affected sections of society where illegal forms of survival were the norm.

Political violence

Not everyone adopted crime as a means of survival, of course. The vast majority of Colombians are neither violent nor dishonest. There are some who believe that injustice and inequalities are the root of their problems, and they have tried to organise against these.

Peasants, for instance, began to organise in the 1970s against their lack of land. Citizens of small towns began to organise protest movements about the lack of services, and Indian groups fought for the return of lands taken from them by the Spanish invaders. Many of these movements have questioned the continued control of political life by the two traditional parties.

The movements have faced violence from local landowners, the army and the police, who fear such challenges. Political violence and human rights violations against protest movements is another kind of violence in Colombia, very different from criminal violence.

Left-wing guerrillas

Some Colombians have adopted violence as a means of bringing about social change. During the 1960s and 1970s, guerrilla movements sprang up in Colombia advocating revolution. These were movements which grew partly out of the frustrations caused by the difficulties of any third party entering the political system. Many young people became disillusioned with elections and they tried to force change through armed struggle.

△ The 14th Battalion of the Colombian Army patrols the streets of San Vicente de Chucuri during the daytime curfew, June 1988. The army's main efforts have been in the counter-insurgency war against the guerrillas and their suspected civilian sympathisers.

▽ Peasants who have been marching for land reform are stopped and searched by the Colombian Army on the pretence that they might be involved with the guerrillas. Many peasants have been victims of army violence, as the army believes their struggle for land means they are subversive.

These groups entered the drugs war scenario for two reasons. The first was that one guerrilla group in particular, the Revolutionary Armed Forces of Colombia (FARC), has protected many of the peasant coca producers against the large landowners and drug traffickers, in return for a tax on the coca grown.

The second reason is that the counter-insurgency war of the army against the guerrillas is often confused with the drugs war. The army is involved in both. Often it has identified any form of protest with armed struggle and the "communist threat" rather than as an expression of a democratic right of people to organise and protest. It has used severe repression against civilian organisations and their leaders, including arrests, torture, "disappearances" and even murder. The link between the drugs war and the counter-insurgency war is that although officially involved in the war against the drug barons, sectors of the armed forces have allied with the barons against the guerrillas and their suspected civilian supporters.

Military response

During the 1980s, the army believed the greatest threat to Colombian society came from the organisers of popular protest and the guerrilla groups rather than from the drug traffickers. It opposed a plan by President Belisario Betancur Cuartas to negotiate peace with the guerrillas.

Sectors of the army were even prepared to ally with the drug traffickers along with the most conservative groups in Colombia to eliminate opposition movements which they considered "subversive". These included banana workers on the plantations of Uraba who were trying to organise a trade union, as well as members and leaders of a new and legal political alliance associated with the Communist Party, known as the Patriotic Union (UP). Over 1,000 UP activists were killed during 1985-90, including its presidential candidate, even though they are committed to peace and electoral politics.

This led to continuous human rights violations throughout the decade, and condemnation from organisations such as Amnesty International. Many of the killings which took place were not organised directly by the army, but by paramilitary groups or death squads, financed by the drug traffickers, in which particular army officers and landowners participated. By the mid-1980s, the government admitted that there were 140 paramilitary groups operating in different regions of the country.

The drugs war

Colombia hit the news when the government finally chose to wage war on the drug barons after the killing of Luis Carlos Galan. The state had already allowed the drug barons to build up their power for over a decade.

Cocaine trafficking in Colombia grew in the late 1970s. It occurred against a background of political crisis and uneven social and economic development, which saw some parts of the economy grow alongside large pockets of misery in the cities and in the countryside.

The cocaine traffickers mostly came out of the criminal culture of the cities, particularly Medellín and Cali. Before getting involved in cocaine, some had been engaged in emerald smuggling and in the marijuana trade. The money generated by cocaine greatly increased the level and nature of violence. For instance, the number of murders using firearms rose in Medellín from 40 per cent in 1979 to 76 per cent in 1985, and in Cali from 51 per cent in 1980 to 85 per cent in 1986. The mafia has used professional assassins, known as the *sicario*, to carry out murders of opponents.

The mafia became major employers in a country where employment opportunities were very limited. It employed people as bodyguards, chauffeurs and servants, as well as in coca processing. Some mafia leaders also became well-known for their "charitable" activities, like building houses and football pitches in the slum areas of the big cities. But the mafia bosses put most of their money into American or European banks, or use it to buy themselves luxuries, such as enormous houses, hotels, casinos, paintings, race horses and so on. They protect their massive profits by maintaining private armies.

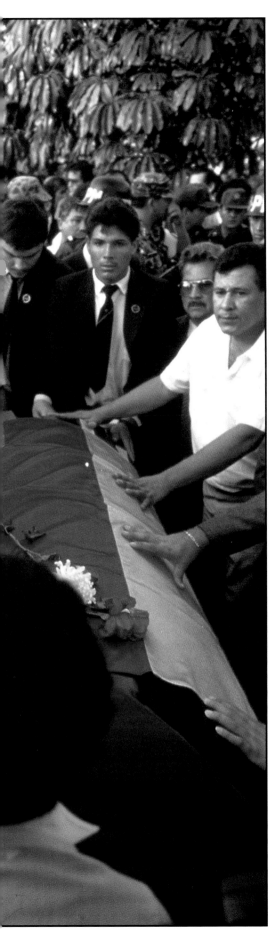

The drug barons' role in politics

The drug barons see themselves as businessmen, and want to be accepted as such in society. Therefore they align themselves with landowners and professional businessmen. They join in attempts to eliminate left-wing political activists in order to increase their standing with the elite.

Some of their money has gone into "buying" politicians and judges. In particular, the mafia has been concerned to prevent the extradition of any of their number to the United States. The mafia's fear of extradition lay behind a number of murders of prominent figures who favoured such a step, or threatened to move against the mafia in a more systematic way than before. Among those killed were a Minister of Justice, Rodrigo Lara Bonilla; an Attorney-General, Carlos Mauro Hoyos Jimenez; and Pardo Leal, leader of the Patriotic Union (UP).

The killing of Liberal Party politician, Luis Carlos Galan, in August 1989 shocked the country. Galan was both committed to destroying the power of the mafia, and to reforming the political institutions of the state, whose weakness had allowed the mafia to grow so powerful in the first place. If he had lived Galan might well have won the 1990 presidential elections. The government could not ignore this assassination, as it was a major challenge to its authority. Following the death of Galan, it launched the most significant offensive yet against the mafia.

◁ The funeral of Carlos Mauro Hoyos Jimenez, former Attorney General, who was kidnapped and killed on the orders of the Medellín cartel in January 1988. He was known to favour strong measures against the drug barons.

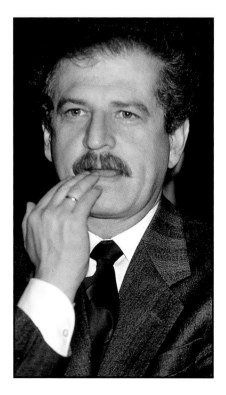

▷ Although a member of the ruling elite, Galan was also a reforming politician. He attacked the corruption of traditional politicians as well as the drug barons. He was the first of three presidential candidates to be killed before the May 1990 elections.

The cocaine war is declared

Immediately after Galan's murder, the government issued an emergency decree and began a sweeping attack on mafia property. Some 11,000 people suspected of being involved in the cocaine business were arrested in the first week of the offensive. Most of them were people on the lower rungs of the ladder of the cocaine trade, and a great many were later released. Property known to belong to the mafia was confiscated and cocaine laboratories were destroyed. Over 1,200 weapons and 900 vehicles and aircraft were seized. The United States gave financial and military aid and demanded the extradition of 12 mafia leaders wanted in order to stand trial in America.

The mafia hit back. They declared that they would kill ten judges for every one of their members extradited. Judges went everywhere under armed guard. The mafia launched a bombing campaign in the major cities at the end of September, targeting the banks, the headquarters of the political parties, commercial centres and schools. The newspaper *El Espectador* was bombed. At the end of November, a bomb destroyed an *Avianca* jet, killing all 107 people on board. In December, another bomb blew up the headquarters of the DAS, the government security agency whose head, General Maza Marquez, was leading the government offensive against the drug barons. The General escaped unharmed although many others were killed.

△ In August 1989 there was fighting on the streets of many Colombian cities as the army moved in on people associated with the drug barons. The estates of the leading drug barons were invaded and there were battles as drug barons' security guards fought the army. By spring 1990 the drugs war had intensified.

Impunity
Colombia's legal system has long been unable to cope with the level of crime in the country. In 1985 only 20 per cent of all crimes were reported in the 11 major towns, and only one per cent of these resulted in a prison sentence. Over 200 judges have been murdered. President Barco has had nine Ministers of Justice. Many resigned in fear of their lives.

The outcome of the cocaine war

At the end of December 1989, the government scored their most notable victory to date, the killing of a leading drugs baron, Gonzalo Rodriguez Gacha. They also managed to have the man reputedly responsible for the Medellín cartel's operations in southern Colombia, Evaristo Porras Ardila, extradited to the United States to stand trial for cocaine trafficking.

But these successes did not destroy the drugs cartels. Most of the leading drug barons survived. The Medellín cartel's operations had been hit, and by February 1990 it was trying to make a deal with the government. But the Cali-based drug cartel, which operated in a quieter way than the one in Medellín, had hardly been touched.

Six months after the cocaine war had been launched, it did not look as if the government was anywhere near ending the cocaine business. At the most it had weakened the operations of the Medellín cartel. But its leaders were still immensely wealthy and still controlled large numbers of armed men. The war against the popular movement had also resumed. Two more presidential candidates were killed in March and April 1990, Bernardo Jaramillo of the UP and Carlos Pizarro, leader of the M-19 guerrilla group which had become a legal political party. These killings were not just the work of the drugs mafia, but of a broad alliance of forces opposed to reform.

△ The drug barons responded to the government's actions against them by a bombing campaign in the major cities.

▽ A leading trafficker, Rodriguez Gacha, was killed by special police units in December 1989.

Solutions: What can be done?

Everyone involved in the drugs war, both in Colombia and the United States, has different ideas on what should be done to solve the drugs problem.

△ Burning cocaine seized during the government's offensive against the drug barons. The offensive has had little effect on supply to the United States.

The drugs war in Colombia exposed a number of conflicting views both within Colombia and outside, on how best to deal with the drugs problem. The different groups involved in the problem – the US government, the Colombian (and Peruvian and Bolivian) governments, the growers, the traffickers themselves, and the Colombian people's organisations – have different ideas.

The United States and the military solution

The US government is mainly concerned to stop the supply of coca and cocaine. It sees the solution to the cocaine problem as the eradication of the coca plant in the areas it is grown and the use of the army against growers and traffickers where necessary.

Latin American governments have collaborated with this approach, though it is very controversial. One of the controversies is over the nature of the eradication programmes. In the mid-1980s the government planned to remove the coca bushes by hand; peasants in Peru, for example, were offered about US$300 to destroy one hectare of coca. But this was rejected by most of the peasants, who often turned to local guerrilla movements for protection. This resulted in attacks on eradication workers and the

United States' strategy changed to involve air raids on cocaine processing laboratories and traffickers' airstrips. This cemented the peasant-guerrilla alliance in the Upper Huallaga valley of Peru and resulted in only a temporary disruption of the cocaine business.

By the late 1980s, the US government began discussing an even more controversial strategy: the use of herbicides sprayed over the coca crops to destroy them. The herbicide chosen was Spike. But the US Environmental Protection Agency asserted that Spike should not be used on wetland areas, and the targeted area of the Upper Huallaga valley included several tropical wet evergreen forests. Spike would remain in the rivers for up to five years, destroying food crops, small birds and animals, and contaminating the Amazon River as well as one of its tributaries, the Huallaga River. Spike had also not been tested for long-term effects, such as birth defects or cancer. The United States had to put the proposal on hold.

The United States has put pressure on the Bolivian government to eradicate coca, threatening to cut off aid if it does not. Under US pressure, the Bolivian congress passed a law in 1988 which made coca cultivation illegal except in a designated area of the Yungas. This resulted in strong protests by the peasants in the Chapare. In one such protest in 1987, six peasants were killed by the army and many others wounded.

Intervention of the US Army

The United States has also increased the role of the US Army in an effort to deal with the problem. In 1986, 160 American soldiers and six Black Hawk helicopters were sent to Bolivia to help Bolivian drugs police destroy cocaine laboratories. This was called Operation Blast Furnace. Another operation was launched in Peru in 1988, called Operation Snowcap, aimed at establishing a permanent US anti-drug presence in the coca-growing regions of Bolivia and Peru. By October 1989, there were about 100 US civilians working in Peru and Bolivia under Operation Snowcap, and some 50 Green Beret military officers.

The presence of US troops in Latin America is also highly controversial. There is a long history of American military intervention in the region, and many Latin Americans are deeply opposed to US soldiers operating on their soil. National feelings run high against attempts by the United States to increase its already highly visible power and influence in the region.

▽ Military supplies from the United States arrive in Colombia, September 1989.

US aid to Colombia

The United States has also put a lot of pressure on the Colombian government to deal with the powerful traffickers. It has demanded the extradition of the most wanted drug barons, and after the murder of Galan, it sent US$65 million as an emergency military package. However, the chief of police complained that the assistance went to the Colombian Army when it was the police that were mostly responsible for dealing with the drugs problem. Many fear that increasing the power of the army will also enhance its ability to repress the local population.

In February 1990, President George Bush offered more financial assistance for the drugs war. The American people are particularly concerned about the drugs problem, and Bush has made it an important theme of his administration. Although he recognises that there is a problem with the demand for cocaine in the United States, the emphasis of US policy is still on dealing with the supply of coca and cocaine by military means.

Within the United States itself, some fear that such a strategy will result in increasing numbers of US troops getting dragged into a prolonged and unwinnable war. Some politicians point out that the flow of cocaine has never been halted for more than a short time. They also say that using military methods to deal with the drugs problem has encouraged peasants in Peru and Colombia to turn to local guerrilla armies for help.

△ The presidents of the main cocaine consumer country (the United States) and the main producers (Peru, Bolivia and Colombia) met in Colombia in February 1990. The conference noted that the drugs problem was one of demand as well as supply but there were no significant results.

Legalising cocaine
Some US politicians believe that ultimately the only solution to the drugs problem is to legalise cocaine. They argue that the cocaine trade is so violent and cocaine commands such a high price because it is illegal. If it were made legal, the price would fall dramatically and the drug barons would lose their power and influence. But many are opposed on moral grounds to making drugs cheaper and more widely available.

Latin American governments

The Latin American governments do not oppose military solutions as such, but put equal or more emphasis on the problem of demand for drugs. They argue that as long as a large market for cocaine exists, there will always be people ready to supply it. They want to see the United States deal with the problems that have created such a demand for drugs in America.

They are also concerned about the impact the eradication of the drug will have on their very fragile economies. The drug provides both employment and an income to many thousands of people which the state has been unable to provide. Without that, the governments could face even greater social unrest than many do already. They are also concerned at the loss of foreign exchange if cocaine production were to end.

The Latin American governments, therefore, argue that if they are to end the production of cocaine, they should be given ample foreign aid to assist the recovery of their economies and generate employment for those who now work for the cocaine mafia. The aid would also go to finance crop substitution programmes for the coca growers (that is, give peasants money to help them switch from coca to another crop) or to investment in other agricultural regions where coca growers could be resettled. They also want easier access to American and other markets for their goods, to enable them to increase their export earnings.

△ Women weep at the loss of loved ones as political and drug-related violence continues to claim many lives in Colombia. Human rights violations against the civilian population increased in 1990, suggesting that right-wing paramilitary violence continues.

There is concern within Colombia at the increasing numbers of cocaine and *basuco* consumers. *Basuco* is an adulterated and highly poisonous form of cocaine base. There are an estimated 300,000 *basuco* addicts in Colombia. But the major problem of consumption is in the United States, where the appetite for drugs of all kinds remains high. There is evidence that many unemployed and poor people in the inner cities are now addicted to crack.

The coca growers

Coca is grown because it enables peasants to earn a better living than any other crop can provide. The problem with solutions aimed at encouraging peasants to switch to other crops is that no other crop provides a comparable income, and that coca thrives in conditions that most other crops cannot survive in: heavy rainfall, rugged terrain and soils high in acids and low in nutrients.

In Peru, 60-70 per cent of total coca production in the Upper Huallaga valley is grown on steep slopes where no other crops can grow. In the Chapare in Bolivia, the land is flatter, but the soils are poor and very heavy rainfall means a short growing season. Some experts have said that if coca were not cultivated in the Chapare, the region could only support one-third of the families who now live there.

Where coca is grown on land that is suitable for some food crops, the coca plant uses up all the soil's essential vitamins and nutrients. In these cases, considerable investment is needed to recover the land. To persuade the growers to give up coca production in the areas where it is currently grown is difficult. Some growers might be persuaded to move to other areas with offers of land and financial help, but such programmes would be very costly. Alternatives for the coca growers will require land reform programmes and the creation of new jobs.

The traffickers – negotiate with us

The Medellín cartel (though not the drug barons of Cali) have offered to negotiate with the Colombian government. They say they will give up the cocaine business in return for the right to return their profits to Colombia and an end to the threat of extradition. There are many in the Colombian political establishment who are prepared to negotiate on these terms, although President Barco declared he would not. Presidential elections held on 27 May 1990 led to the election of Liberal candidate César Gaviria, who supports continuation of the drugs war.

Colombia's people's organisations

Activists in Colombia's popular movements, who have been targeted by the army and cocaine-funded death squads, are also anxious to see an end to the cocaine industry and the power of the drug barons. For them the solution should not involve strengthening the Colombian Army, which has been involved with the death squads. Nor should it involve increased US involvement in the country,

△ Bolivian coca growers are incensed at attempts to take away their livelihood and have formed an organisation to defend their rights.

The issue of negotiations with the drug traffickers is a very sensitive one in Colombia. The US government is clearly totally opposed to them, but many Colombians feel holding talks is the only way to stop the violence. In October 1989, newspapers revealed that indirect talks had taken place between the government and traffickers before Galan's assassination.

as the United States is the source of counter-insurgency training and ideas which have encouraged the local army to seek military solutions to social unrest. For them the solution lies in a more equal society. The poverty of rural and urban communities is the root of the problem, and only by dealing with issues such as access to land and jobs can it be resolved.

They would also argue that similar problems of deprivation in the inner cities of the United States and Europe have led to the drugs problem. What is needed is government spending on drug education, treatment services and social welfare, as well as measures to create more jobs. The problem of cocaine, they argue, cannot be solved by military or punitive means either in Latin America or in the United States.

△ Crack smokers in the Bronx. Crack consumption is having a terrible effect on community and family life as drug-related violence in America increases.

▽ In 1982 Los Angeles police displayed the results of a drug bust: 40 kg of cocaine worth US$26 million, US$402,000 in cash and three handguns. In 1989 the US government set aside US$2.5 billion for a five-year programme of economic, military, law enforcement and intelligence aid in the three Andean countries.

Geography and economy

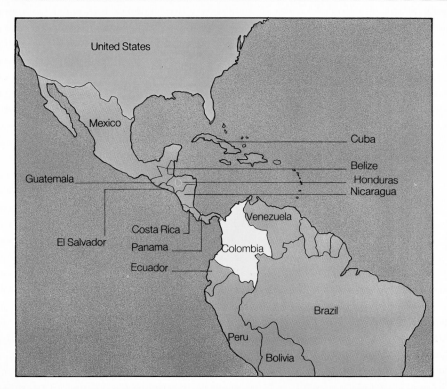

Colombia's two economies

Colombia is a Third World country. This means that the level of wealth created is nowhere near that of the First World (eg the United States, Western Europe, Japan) or even the Second World (the Soviet Union and Eastern Europe). However, Colombia is not as poor as most African and many Asian countries. It is sometimes called a middle-income country. Colombia, nevertheless, shares with other Third World countries economic vulnerability and uncertainty because of its dependence on exports of mostly raw materials whose prices go up and down constantly according to world demand, and also its massive foreign debt.

Despite a considerable degree of economic growth since 1958, the fruits of that growth have been very unevenly distributed. The process of growth has brought massive social changes and has created two economies which are related: a modern and fairly prosperous economy and also a backward and poor one, in which the majority of the population live and work. The government's figures show that at least 40 per cent of Colombia's population, about 12 million people, live in poverty.

The "modern" economy...

In the "modern" sector, industries produce textiles, foods and drinks, and also paper products, chemicals and even cars. Colombia has also managed to create a "modern" agricultural sector. Gradually Colombia has shifted from almost total dependence on

Colombia is the fourth largest country in South America (1.14 million square km), it is also the third most populated country in the region (30.8 million people in 1988) and has the fifth largest economy (gross domestic product per person US$1,372). It borders on Panama, Venezuela, Ecuador, Peru and Brazil. It is a gateway to the south of Latin America, with coastlines on the Caribbean Sea and Pacific Ocean.

Colombia is a mosaic of different regions. Daunting physical barriers of mountains, rivers and jungles limit communication between regions. As a result, Colombia's regions each have a distinct pattern of cultural, social and economic development. There are still vast areas of the country which are isolated and abandoned by central government, another important factor in understanding the growth of the drug trade.

Population distribution

The most heavily populated region is the west, which is dominated by the three mountain ranges of the Andes. These ranges are cut by the deep valleys of the Magdalena and Cauca rivers. This region covers 26 per cent of the country's surface but 80 per cent of its population live there, and it is the geographic centre of the country's economic life.

The eastern region is made up of large expanses of flat grassy plains, or savannas, to its north, and scarcely populated forests and part of the Amazon jungle to the south. Only two per cent of the population inhabit this area.

There is a third region which is shaped by the Caribbean and Pacific coasts and the Caribbean coastal plain. It covers 19 per cent of the national territory and 19 per cent of the population are settled there.

Economic differences between cocaine producers and takers

The difference in the level of development of the drug-producing nations and the major consuming nations can be seen from these figures from the 1989 World Bank's World Development report. It states that the Gross National Product (GNP) per person of cocaine producers is: Bolivia $580, Colombia $1,240 and Peru $1,470. The per person GNP of cocaine consumers is: United States $18,530 and Britain $10,420.

coffee exports, and today exports a range of agricultural goods including bananas and flowers. Coffee exports still represent a third of all exports, and any fall in its price seriously affects the economy. Colombia has also developed its considerable energy resources, though it has had to depend on foreign companies and foreign loans, as it lacks the huge sums required for expensive coal, oil and hydroelectric projects. These projects have created a large foreign debt. Colombia's oil and coal exports have also been hit by low world prices for most of the 1980s.

In common with most other Third World countries, Colombia has had most difficulty in developing its exports of industrial goods, though these command much higher prices than raw materials.

Anyone who visits Colombia would immediately recognise this "modern" sector. The northern part of the capital city, Bogotá, has gleaming office blocks, impressive banking complexes, well-stocked shopping arcades and supermarkets, and luxury apartment buildings.

The poor in the cities

The southern part of Bogotá, however, offers a very different picture. Here the housing is poor, in some places just shacks. The people mostly use paraffin for cooking, and everywhere there are people selling on the streets. Many people have to survive on theft and crime.

Colombia has many cities and towns like this. In many smaller towns there is no running water in the poor districts and no sewerage, the roads are unpaved and there is no street lighting. Colombia has a chronic housing shortage and many people live in slums, shacks and shanty-towns.

Today, most Colombians live in cities and towns. People flooded into the towns because there was not enough land for them to support their families in the countryside. The move from city to countryside took place very rapidly: whereas 40 per cent lived in the towns in 1951, by 1987 70 per cent lived there. The people who came into the towns needed work but there was not enough industry to employ people.

So people had to make a living on the streets in any way they could, in casual jobs or small workshops. There is no state control of this sector of the economy, and it is known as the "informal" sector. Incomes are low and there is very little security for those who work in the informal sector.

...and in the countryside

For those who remained in the countryside, poverty and deprivation are even more acute. The struggle for land has continued in Colombia. Peasant farmers try to survive on small plots where they do not make enough money to improve their land. Others have been made landless by the expansion of large cattle ranchers or wealthier landowners.

Many peasants have left their traditional homes to colonise the sparsely populated lowland areas. But they have no money. The state has given almost no assistance, so they settle in areas without proper roads, and with no electricity or running water. The peasants cut down the trees to clear a plot of land in order to grow the food they need. Often they have to borrow money from moneylenders to buy basic necessities, promising in return to give any surplus crops they produce. If the harvest fails, the farmer is in debt and may have to give up his land to the moneylender.

Soon after the peasant colonisers come the large cattle ranchers who want to take over the land cleared by the peasants. There is a lot of violence, as the cattle barons sometimes use the police and their own private armies to evict the peasants. It is in these areas that the peasants began growing coca in the late 1970s, a crop which guaranteed an income thus helping them to defend themselves against the large landowners.

31

Cocaine facts

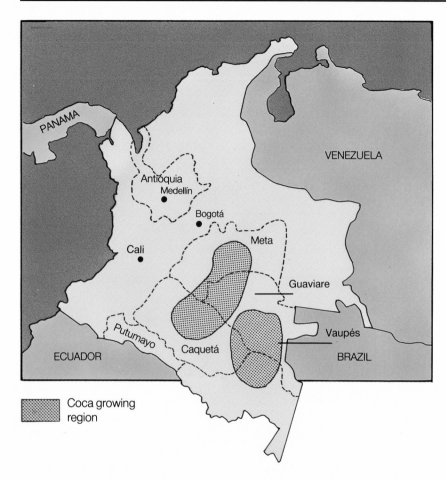

PANAMA

VENEZUELA

Antióquia
Medellín

Bogotá

Cali

Meta

Guaviare

Putumayo

Vaupés

Caquetá

ECUADOR

BRAZIL

Coca growing
region

Where is it grown?
Over four-fifths of South American coca originates in Peru and Bolivia; Peru is by far the world's largest producer. Coca is grown in 14 of Peru's 24 departments, or provinces. The two most important areas, responsible for 90 per cent of the country's cultivation and production, are the Upper Urubamba valley, and most notably, the Upper Huallaga valley between the towns of Panao and Campanilla, about 400-700 miles north-east of Lima, the capital.

The latter region is almost totally dependent on coca for its farm income. Estimates for the number of peasant families who grow coca in the Upper Huallaga valley range from 60-300,000 as compared to

10-20,000 elsewhere. The US Department of State estimates that 100,000 hectares of land are devoted to coca in Peru, of which 85,000 are in the Upper Huallaga valley.

In Bolivia most production is in the Chapare and Yungas region in the departments of Cochabamba and La Paz respectively. The Chapare produces 75-80 per cent of Bolivia's coca, and this area of subtropical rainforest is almost wholly dependent on coca production. An estimated 80,000 families are involved in coca production in Bolivia on 40- 60,000 hectares of land.

In Colombia, the coca plant is cultivated mainly in the remote plains, or *llanos*, and jungle regions of southeastern and southern Colombia, in the

departments of Meta, Guaviare and Vaupés, Caquetá and Putumayo. The quality of Colombian coca is not as good as that of its neighbours.

How is it made?
Cocaine is relatively easy to make and can be done in basic laboratories. The process takes place in three stages.

First, the coca leaves are mashed and soaked in a solution of kerosene or gasoline and sodium carbonate to remove the narcotic alkaloid. In Peru and Bolivia, 300-500 kg of leaves make about one kg of cocaine. (In Colombia it takes more leaves to make one kg of cocaine because the cocaine content of Colombian leaves is about half that of Peruvian or Bolivian leaves.) This produces a coca paste which is about 40 per cent pure cocaine.

Secondly, the paste is treated with sulphuric acid and potassium permanganate to form a cocaine base which is 90-92 per cent pure cocaine.

Finally, ether and acetone are used to convert the base into cocaine hydrochloride, the purest form of the drug. This is then diluted, or "cut," with sugar or lactose for sale on the street by dealers.

Why is it grown?
The most important reason for growing coca is economic. No other crop could give a similar income to the peasants who grow it – growing coca for export makes more money than growing crops for local consumption. But there are other factors too.

All the regions where coca is grown share common features.

They are isolated regions, which have been colonised in the last few decades by peasants who could not make a living on their existing plots. The state has offered very little support to the peasants and the regions are all characterised by government neglect. Communication with the outside world is very poor. It is a ten-hour drive from Lima to the first urban centre of the Upper Huallaga valley. Many coca-growing areas of Colombia are hundreds of miles from urban centres, and the traffickers use planes to transport the coca. The communication problems and the small size of local markets make it difficult to develop commercial agriculture.

Limited alternatives

There are very few alternative means for making a living in all three countries. Bolivia's gross national product (the total monetary value of everything produced in a country) declined by 2.3 per cent per year from 1980 to 1986, while coca production annually grew an estimated 35 per cent each of those years.

Official unemployment tripled from 1980 to 1986 (from 5.7 per cent to 20 per cent), the same amount as the number of families said to be involved in coca production. When the price of tin collapsed in 1985,

some 20,000 tin miners lost their jobs and an estimated 5,000 of these sought work as *pisadores* in the Chapare. The official unemployment rates, in Peru and Bolivia as well as Colombia, do not portray a true picture of lack of job opportunities.

In Colombia land is distributed very unequally, and the growth of big commercial estates, for crops like coffee and bananas, has thrown many peasants off the land. This has forced peasants to migrate either to the shanty-towns outside the major cities or else to the areas of colonisation. Most people work in the "informal" sector, where they scratch a meagre living on the streets anyway they can, rather than in a proper job where pay and conditions are regulated by the state.

Who earns what?

Huge profits can be made from cocaine, but who really benefits? The table below illustrates the relative profits made at each stage of the transformation of the coca leaf to street cocaine. It shows that what the peasant earns from growing the coca leaf is a very small fraction of its street value. But for the impoverished peasant communities it represents a cash income that they could not earn otherwise.

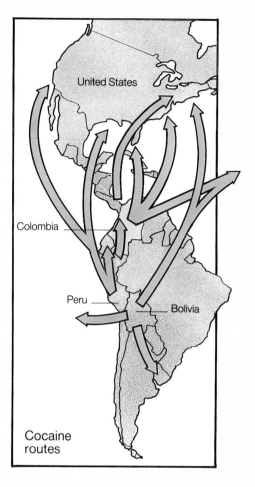

Cocaine routes

Many spend it on consumer goods, leading to such ironies as the peasants of the Colombian coca region who buy fridges when there is no electricity supply. Some have a longer term view and spend it on improving their land.

The FARC guerrillas in Colombia have encouraged the peasants in the coca-growing areas they control to grow food crops as well as coca.

BOLIVIA/PERU		COLOMBIA		UNITED STATES
coca leaf	coca paste	cocaine base	chlorohydrate of cocaine	street cocaine
500 kg	2.5 kg	1 kg	1 kg	8 kg
$1000	$5000	$11,000	$20-60,000 *	$500,000

* In its purest form, cocaine chlorohydrate worth US $60,000 per kg

Chronology

Colombia's history since the Spanish conquest has been characterised by violence. The Spaniards and their descendants exploited the Indians and the African people they used as slaves. After the war of independence, the new Colombian state was weak and violence and civil war alternated with periods of peaceful government. However the gulf between the rich and the powerless poor grew and led to another period of civil war. When peace was restored, Colombia enjoyed rapid economic growth.

1509 Spanish found San Sebastián de Uraba.

1781 Uprising of the Comunero movement.

1810-1816 Wars of Independence.

1819 Bolivar's triumphant entry into Bogotá.

1830 Bolivar dies.

1899-1902 Thousand Day War.

1903 United States stirs up Panamanian separatism in order to build canal.

1934-1938 President Lopez Pumarejo's "revolution on the march".

1948 Jorge Eliécer Gaitán, Liberal Party populist leader, assassinated.

1948-1953 Worst years of civil war known as *La Violencia*.

1953-1957 Military government of Rojas Pinilla.

1958-1964 Second phase of *La Violencia*.

1958 National Front of Liberal and Conservative Parties established.

1979 Marijuana production stamped out in Colombia's Caribbean coastal region. Cocaine trade growing rapidly.

1981 First cocaine-funded death squad appears; the MAS.

1983 Amnesty International denounces 800 extrajudicial political killings attributed to members of the army, police and paramilitary groups.

1984 Drug barons kill the Minister of Justice, Rodrigo Lara Bonilla.

1985 The Colombian Supreme Court suspends the extradition treaty with the United States. President Belisario Betancur's peace initiative with guerrillas collapses.

1986 President Barco comes into office. For the first time his government rules without the participation of (Conservative) opposition. Political killings and massacres increase over next few years; an estimated 8,000 people die 1986-89.

1988 Attorney-General Carlos Mauro Hoyos kidnapped and killed by drug barons.

August 1989 Liberal politician, Luis Carlos Galan, assassinated. Government renews extradition treaty and launches most sustained offensive yet against drugs mafia.

September 1989 Mafia bombing campaign in major cities.

November 1989 Mafia bomb destroys *Avianca* plane, killing 107 people.

December 1989 Bomb blows up DAS headquarters. Leading drug baron, Rodriguez Gacha, killed. The war against the popular movement intensifies following a brief respite at the height of the drugs war. Ramon Emilio Arcila, a lawyer, leader of the civic movement of Antioquia, is shot dead.

February 1990 Colombian, Peruvian and Bolivian presidents meet US President Bush in Cartagena, Colombia, to discuss drugs issue. Medellín cartel offers to negotiate.

March 1990 Bernardo Jaramillo, presidential candidate and leader of the Patriotic Union (UP) is killed in Bogotá airport as he was about to go on holiday. UP then announced it was pulling out of the presidential elections of May 1990 due to the murder of its candidate and the lack of freedom to carry out their campaign.

April 1990 Drug summit held in London. Carlos Pizarro is shot dead. He was the leader of the former guerrilla movement M-19, now a legal party, and its presidential candidate.

Statistics and Glossary

Land area: 1,141,748 sq km
Population (1988) 30.8 million
Annual growth rate 1.7 per cent
Urban (1987) 69.1 per cent
Bogotá 4.20 million
Medellín 2.69 million
Cali 1.65 million

The people:
(approximate ethnic composition)
Mestizos (mixed Spanish and Indian) 70 per cent
European 22 per cent
Amerindian 2 per cent
African 6 per cent

Language: Spanish
Religion: Catholic 96 per cent

Literacy: 88 per cent (1987)
Secondary education – percentage of age group in secondary education: 56 per cent (1986)

Health: Infant mortality (per 1,000 live births) 46 (1987)
Life expectancy at birth 66 (1987)
Malnutrition: 20 per cent of children under five suffer from malnutrition and a further 19.7 per cent are at risk. (There are however many regional differences with all these figures. The Choco is one of the most backward departments, for instance, and here life

expectancy is 47 years and 144 children die in every 1,000 live births)

The economy:
Principal exports, percentage of total 1988:
Coffee 32.6 per cent
Petroleum and derivatives 19.6 per cent
Textiles, clothing, leather and footwear 6.6 per cent
Coal 6.1 per cent
Bananas 5 per cent
Chemical products 4.2 per cent
Flowers 3.8 per cent

Cocaine is an alkaloid obtained from coca leaves. It is used as an anaesthetic and illegally as a narcotic drug.

Coup d'etat is the overthrow of a government, usually by the armed forces.

Crack is a form of cocaine which can be smoked and is highly addictive.

Creoles are the descendants of Europeans, born in Latin America.

Democracy is a form of government in which people have a say, usually by electing representatives.

Drug baron is the name given to the person in charge of a large drug manufacturing or distribution network. Drug barons are often very rich because of the illegal and high profits to be made out of drugs.

Extradition is the delivery of criminals by one country to another so that they can face trial for crimes committed in that country.

Falangist is the name of the extreme right-wing party which gained power in Spain in the 1930s under Franco.

Guerrilla is an armed rebel who joins a group, usually to fight against an army or government which is in power.

Latifundia Latin for "wide estate". Usually refers to huge landed estates in Italy, Spain or Latin America, where many people are employed to work the land.

La Violencia means "the violence" and is the name given to the period of civil war in Colombia from 1948 to 1964. The worst period of violence was 1948-57.

Mafia is the name of any secret criminal organisation. This form of criminal activity started in Sicily. Sicilians brought the mafia to the United States and this form of organisation has since spread throughout the world. Mafias control the illegal drugs trade.

Marijuana is an illegal drug that has an intoxicating effect. It is made from the dried leaves of the cannabis plant and is often smoked in cigarettes.

Narcotic means a substance which affects the central nervous system. It can produce sleepiness, relaxation and sometimes dizziness.

Oligarchy is a small group of very wealthy people who govern a city or state.

Traffickers are people who buy and sell drugs, or receive and distribute them for profit.

Index

Africans 8, 9
aid 26, 27
air strips 25
Amnesty International 19
Antioquia 13

banks 20
Barco Vargas, President
    Virgilio 15, 19, 22, 28
basuco 27
Battle of Boyaca 10
Betancur Cuartas,
    President Belisario 19
Bogotá 14, 16, 17, 31
"*Bogotazo*" 14
Bolivar, Simon 10
Bolivia 5, 6, 24, 25, 28, 32,
    33
bombing 22, 23
Boyaca 17
bribery 6, 17
Britain 6, 7
Bush, President George 26

caciques 12
Cali 20, 23, 28
Camargo estate 12
Catholic Church 10, 11, 14
Ceilan 14
Chapare 6, 25, 28
Ciénaga massacre 13
cities 17, 20, 22, 23, 31
civil wars 10, 11, 14
coca 4-6, 12, 19, 25, 26,
    28, 31, 32
coca growers 6, 12, 24, 27,
    28, 31, 32
coca processing 19, 20,
    28, 32
Coca-Cola 5
cocaine 17, 20, 24, 26, 27,
    32, 33, 35
cocaine production 5, 6,
    27
coffee 12, 13, 31
Colombian Army 5, 10, 14,
    15, 18, 19, 22, 26, 28, 29

Communist Party 19
Conservative Party 10-16
counter-insurgency 18, 29
crack 6, 7, 27, 35
Creoles 9, 10, 35
criminal violence 16
crop substitution
    programmes 27, 28

DAS 22

de Roux, Francisco 10
death squads 19, 27, 28
demand for cocaine 5, 7,
    26, 27, 29
drug barons 7, 16, 21-23,
    26, 28, 35
drug traffickers 19, 23-28,
    35
drugs trade 5, 6, 17, 22
drugs war 2, 19-24, 26

economic growth 13-16,
    17, 30
economy 9, 10, 12, 27, 30,
    31
El Espectador 22
elections 14, 15, 18, 21,
    23, 28
emeralds 17, 20
Environmental Protection
    Agency 25
eradication programmes
    24, 25, 27
Escobar, Pablo 6, 7
export crops 11-13
exports 27, 31
extradition 21-23, 26, 28,
    35

falangists 14, 35
financial aid 22, 26
Franco, Francisco 14

Gacha, Gonzalo Rodriguez
    23
Gaitán, Jorge Eliécer 14
Galan, Luis Carlos 2, 21,
    22, 26, 28
geography 30
gold 13, 17
government, Colombian 7,
    11, 17, 21-24, 26, 28
Green Berets 25
Guambiano people 5
guerrillas 14, 18, 19, 24,
    25, 26, 33, 35

herbicides 25
Holmes, Sherlock 5
human rights violations 18,
    19, 27

Incas 4, 8
income 6, 27, 28, 30, 32
independence 9-11
Indians 8, 9, 18

Jaramillo, Bernardo 23

judiciary 6, 16, 17, 21, 22

La Violencia 14, 15, 35
laboratories 6, 22, 25, 32
landowners 10, 12, 13, 15,
    18, 19, 21, 31
Lara Bonilla, Rodrigo 21
latifundia 12, 13, 35
Latin American
    governments 27
Leal, Pardo 21
left-wing political
    movements 18-23, 28,
    29
legalising cocaine 26
Liberal Party 2, 10-16, 21

M-19 guerrilla group 23
mafia 20-23, 27, 35
marijuana 5, 20, 35
Mauro Hoyos Jimenez,
    Carlos 21
Maza Marquez, General 22
Medellín 20, 23
Medellín cartel 6, 21, 23,
    28
military aid 22, 26
military solution 24-27, 29
murders 17, 20, 21

National Front 15
National Reconstruction,
    government of 11
negotiations 28
New York 6
Nuñez, Rafael 11

Ochoa clan 6
Ochoa, Jorge Luis 6, 7
oligarchy 14, 35
Operation Blast Furnace
    25
Operation Snowcap 25
opportunities 20

Panama 11
Panama Canal 11
Panao 32
paramilitary groups 19
Patriotic Union (Union
    Patriotica) 19, 21, 23
peasants 6, 9, 10, 12, 13,
    15, 18, 19, 24-26, 28, 31,
    32
people's organisations 28,
    29
Peru 4-6, 8, 9, 24, 25, 28,
    32, 33

pisadores 6
Pizarro, Carlos 23
Pizzaro, Francisco 9
police 18, 26
political reform 2, 12, 15,
    21, 23
political violence 16, 18, 19
politics 10, 11, 13-15, 19,
    21
Popayán 9
population 8, 30
Porras Ardila, Evaristo 23
poverty 9, 11, 17, 29, 31
presidential elections 2,
    15, 21, 23, 28
prices 7, 26
private armies 20, 23
profits 6, 7, 20, 28, 33
Pumarejo, President Lopez
    14

Revolutionary Armed
    Forces of Colombia
    (FARC) 19, 33
Rojas Pinilla, General
    Gustavo 15

San Sebastián de Uraba 9
Santa Fe de Bogotá 9
Santa Marta 5
Sicario 20
smuggling 20
social welfare 14, 17
Spain 8-10, 12, 14, 18
Spanish conquest 4, 5,
    8-10
Spike 25
statistics 35

Thatcher, Margaret 7
Thousand Day War 11, 13
trade unions 13, 19, 21

unemployment 27, 28, 33
United States 5, 7, 11,
    21-29, 31
United States Army 25, 26
Upper Huallaga valley 6,
    25, 28, 32, 33
Upper Urubamba valley 32

Viceroyalty of New
    Granada 9
violence 16-20, 27, 28

World Bank 13

Yungas 25

Photographic Credits:
Cover, page 22 and back cover: Susan Mieselas/Magnum;
intro page and page 29 top: Associated Press/Topham;
pages 5 top, 6, 16 both, 17, 20, 21, 23 both, 24 bottom, 26
and 27: Rex Features; pages 4 bottom and 28: F. Scianna/
Magnum; pages 7 top, 15 bottom and 24 top: Frank
Spooner; page 7 bottom: David Browne; pages 8 top and
10: The Mansell Collection; pages 8 bottom, 14, 15 top and
29 bottom: Topham Picture Library; pages 12, 13 and 18
top: Popperfoto; page 18 bottom: Magnum Photo Library.